A HMONG FAMILY

A HMONG FAMILY

By Nora Murphy

Lerner Publications Company • Minneapolis

The interviews for this book were conducted in 1995.

This book is available in two editions:
Library binding by Lerner Publications Company
Soft cover by First Avenue Editions
241 First Avenue North
Minneapolis, MN 55401
ISBN: 0-8225-3406-1 (lib. bdg.)
ISBN: 0-8225-9756-X (pbk.)

A pronunciation guide can be found on page 62.

LIBRARY OF CONGRESS CATALOGING-IN-PUBLICATION DATA

Murphy, Nora.
   A Hmong family / Nora Murphy.
      p. cm. — (Journey between two worlds)
   Includes bibliographical references and index.
   Summary: Depicts the history and culture of the Hmong, a unique ethnic group living in Southeast Asia, and describes the experiences of a Hmong family who left Laos to rebuild their lives in America. Includes a Hmong folktale.
   ISBN 0-8225-3406-1 (lib. bdg. : alk. paper)
   1. Hmong American families—Minnesota—Minneapolis—Case studies—Juvenile literature. 2. Hmong Americans—Minnesota—Minneapolis—Case studies—Juvenile literature. 3. Refugees, Political—Minnesota—Minneapolis—Case studies—Juvenile literature. 4. Refugees, Political—Asia, Southeastern—Case studies—Juvenile literature. 5. Minneapolis (Minn.)—Social life and customs—Juvenile literature. [1. Hmong (Asian people). 2. Hmong Americans. 3. Refugees.] I. Title. II. Series.
F614.M59H5568   1997
305.895—dc20   96-13533

Manufactured in the United States of America
1 2 3 4 5 6 – SP – 02 01 00 99 98 97

AUTHOR'S NOTE

This book would not have been possible without the help, support, and understanding of the entire Vang family—Toua, Kao, Xia, KaYing, Teng, Toukee, Nancy, and especially Xiong Pao Vang and his grandmother, Dou Vue. Thank you for sharing your amazing and triumphant stories. I would also like to thank David Hall and Margie Boler for their helpful comments on the manuscript.

FAMILY'S NOTE

The Vang family would like to express our deep thanks to our sponsors, Mr. Xia Kao Lee and Mrs. Teng Xiong, Kao's sister and her husband. Without them our family would not have been able to get into the United States.

We would also like to thank our relatives in Minnesota—especially Mr. Za Moua Xiong, Kao's father, and all our cousins—who helped our family get settled in our newest home.

Finally we thank the author and the editors for helping us share our family's story.

Hmong refugees (above) *rest at a refugee camp in northeastern Thailand. At its peak in the mid-1980s, Ban Vinai* (facing page) *housed more than 45,000 Hmong, half of whom were under the age of 18. Most of the camp's residents were waiting for permission to move to the United States.*

SERIES INTRODUCTION

 What they have left behind is sometimes a living nightmare of war and hunger that most Americans can hardly begin to imagine. As refugees set out to start a new life in another country, they are torn by many feelings. They may wish they didn't have to leave their homeland. They may fear giving up the only life they have ever known. Many may also feel excitement and hope as they struggle to build a better life in a new country.

People who move from one place to another are called migrants. Two types of migrants are immigrants and refugees. Immigrants choose to leave their homelands, usually to improve their standards of living. They may be leaving behind poverty, famine (hunger), or a failing economy. They may be pursuing a better job or reuniting with family members.

Refugees, on the other hand, often have no choice but to flee their homeland to protect their own personal safety. How could anyone be in so much danger?

A Lao girl stands beside a pile of bombshells, left behind from the country's violent civil war.

The government of his or her country is either unable or unwilling to protect its citizens from persecution, or cruel treatment. In many cases, the government is actually the cause of the persecution. Government leaders or another group within the country may be persecuting anyone of a certain race, religion, or ethnic background. Or they may persecute those who belong to a particular social group or who hold political opinions that are not accepted by the government.

From the 1950s through the mid-1970s, the number of refugees worldwide held steady at between 1.5 and 2.5 million. The number began to rise sharply in 1976. By the mid-1990s, it approached 20 million. These figures do not include people who are fleeing disasters such as famine (estimated to be at least 10 million). Nor do they include those who are forced to leave their homes but stay within their own countries (about 27 million).

As this rise in refugees and other migrants continues, countries that have long welcomed newcomers are beginning to close their doors. Some U.S. citizens question whether the United States should accept refugees when it cannot even meet the needs of all its own people. On the other hand, experts point out that the number of refugees is small—less than 20 percent of all migrants worldwide—so refugees really don't have a very big impact on the nation. Still others suggest that the tide of refugees could be slowed through greater efforts to address the problems that force people to flee. There are no easy answers in this ongoing debate.

This book is one in a series called *Journey Between Two Worlds*, which looks at the lives of refugee families—their difficulties and triumphs. Each book describes the journey of a family from their homeland to the United States and how they adjust to a new life in America while still preserving traditions from their homeland. The series makes no attempt to join the debate about refugees. Instead, *Journey Between Two Worlds* hopes to give readers a better understanding of the daily struggles and joys of a refugee family.

Like the Vangs, most Hmong refugees making the journey to the United States had to leave behind many family members and friends.

"When my dad was 11 years old, like me, he used to carry an M16 assault rifle," says Xiong Pao Vang. Xiong, a sixth-grade student in Minneapolis, Minnesota, is taking a break from playing tag with his younger brothers at a city park.

After checking to see that his little sisters are still on the nearby swings, Xiong continues. "Yeah, my dad had to go out on patrol two or three times a week with a couple of other guys. They'd walk around all night to protect their village from enemy attacks."

Xiong and his family are Hmong, an ethnic group from Asia. In 1986, when Xiong was three years old, the Vangs came to the United States as refugees to escape the danger in the family's homeland of Laos.

Xiong Pao Vang runs through a park in Minneapolis, Minnesota.

The Hmong people traditionally live in the mountainous and forested lands of northern and central Laos.

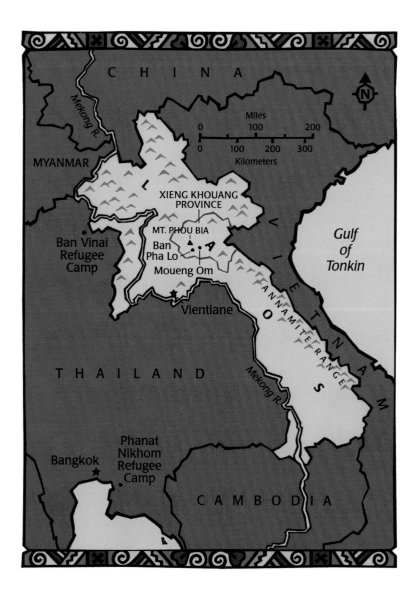

Laos is a mountainous, landlocked country in Southeast Asia. The weather is warm and wet, and nearly two-thirds of the country is covered with rain forests. Laos's northern neighbor is China and to the northwest is Myanmar. The lengthy Mekong River separates Laos from Thailand to the west. Across the Annamite Range to the east lies the country of Vietnam. Laos's neighbor to the south is Cambodia.

During the 1960s, war broke out in Laos. The Pathet Lao (Lao who favored a Communist form of government) fought Lao who were against Communism. The United States was also against Communism and decided to help the anti-Communists in Laos. The United

Rugged mountains and thick rain forests line parts of the Mekong River in north central Laos.

Xiong pushes his sister Nancy on a swing. As the oldest of six children, he often takes care of his younger brothers and sisters.

States organized Hmong soldiers to fight against the Pathet Lao. By 1975 the Communists had won. But under the new Communist government in Laos, life remained dangerous for anyone who had fought against the Pathet Lao. Many Hmong families fled to the United States, which had promised to accept the refugees.

Getting to the United States wasn't easy. After escaping Laos, Hmong families had to cross the Mekong River into neighboring Thailand. There, they waited in refugee camps until they received official permission to enter the United States.

"I didn't have to make the long walk out of Laos to the refugee camp in Thailand," says Xiong, giving his sister Nancy a push on the swing. "But both my parents did. It was really dangerous."

Today Xiong and his family are far away from the dangers and hardships they once knew. "Now that we've moved here to America, we're safe," explains Xiong as he leads his brothers and sisters to an ice-cream truck. "We don't have to fight anymore."

The Vangs live on the first floor of a two-family house in a quiet neighborhood in Minneapolis. Xiong's parents work full-time. His father, Toua, is employed at a Hmong community organization. His mother, Kao, has a job at a telecommunications company. Xiong has five younger brothers and sisters—

Teng, Toukee, KaYing, Kao, Xiong, Nancy, Xia, and Toua Vang relax at home.

Xia (10), twins KaYing and Teng (9), Toukee (7), and Nancy (5). Xiong's grandmother and his uncle's family live upstairs.

Xiong knows that his parents and many other Hmong have fought hard to keep Hmong freedom alive for his generation. "But being Hmong in America isn't always easy," says Xiong. "It can be confusing when you speak Hmong and act Hmong at home and then speak English and act American at school.

"But I guess I'm lucky," he reflects. "When my grandmother was my age, the Hmong were fighting against the Japanese. When my parents were my age, the Hmong were fighting against the Communists. All I have to do is go to school and take care of my younger brothers and sisters!"

 Until recently the Hmong did not have a written language. They kept their history and culture alive through storytelling and passing information by word of mouth. One story says that the Hmong originally came from a place that was frozen and dark for half the year. Some people believe this may have been northern Europe. No matter where they came from originally, most Hmong agree their ancestors traveled by foot to Mongolia (a region of east central Asia) thousands of years ago.

In 2,500 B.C., the Chinese invaded Mongolia. The Hmong moved to the Yellow River valley in northeastern China, where they could keep the freedom to speak their own language and farm their own land. Freedom has always been important to the Hmong. In fact, the word *Hmong* means "free man."

Around 251 B.C., another group of Chinese invaded the Yellow River region. To protect their freedom, the Hmong moved again. This time they traveled southwest to the Yangtze River, where they grew abundant crops of rice along the waterway.

Living peacefully with the Chinese wasn't easy. Conflict over land and taxes was common. The Chinese stole Hmong land, burned Hmong villages, and killed thousands of Hmong people. One story tells of a huge war that started when the Hmong refused to give a young woman to a Chinese warrior.

Agricultural workers in ancient China plant rice and water the field. Early Hmong farmers were among the first people in history to use irrigation (watering) systems to grow rice crops.

Children in Laos and other Southeast Asian countries attended French schools when France controlled the region from the 1800s until the mid-1900s.

In the mid-1800s, the Hmong rose up against the Chinese. But the rebellion didn't stop the hardships. A small group of Hmong realized they would never be free in China. This group, which included Xiong's ancestors, left China. They headed to Southeast Asia, where they settled high in the rugged, jungle-covered mountains of Vietnam, Laos, and Thailand.

About 100 years later, war broke out in Laos and Vietnam, which were controlled by France at that time. The Southeast Asians began fighting for their independence from France. The struggle became part of a larger conflict in Southeast Asia between Communists and anti-Communists. In the United States, this conflict was known as the Vietnam War.

The United States sent troops to fight Communist forces in Vietnam but not in Laos. Instead the United States Central Intelligence Agency (CIA) secretly organized thousands of Hmong foot soldiers to fight against the Pathet Lao (Lao Communists). The Hmong were sometimes called the CIA Secret Army because the U.S. government didn't tell the American people about the fighting in Laos for many years.

Thousands of Hmong men and boys—including Xiong's grandfather and many of his uncles—fought the Pathet Lao under the leadership of Hmong general Vang Pao. The CIA also organized U.S. pilots to attack the Lao Communist forces from the air. The pilots dropped food, medicine, and military supplies for the Hmong as well.

The United States was unable to defeat the Communists in Southeast Asia. In 1975 U.S. troops withdrew from the region, and the Communists in Vietnam and Laos declared victory. After the war, the Pathet Lao set up a Communist government in Laos. The Communists believed in sharing the country's resources equally among all citizens, no matter how hard a person worked.

The United States enlisted many Hmong youths to fight against the Pathet Lao Communists in Laos.

Pathet Lao soldiers take a break. The Pathet Lao mistreated and killed many Hmong families in Laos, causing thousands of Hmong to flee the country in the 1970s and 1980s.

But the Pathet Lao didn't trust the Lao and the Hmong who had supported the United States. Between 1975 and 1980, the Pathet Lao waged a war against these people. This meant that the Hmong, including Xiong's family, were in danger.

The Pathet Lao took Hmong land and dropped chemical weapons from the air, killing many Hmong and destroying their villages and crops. The Pathet Lao also forced Hmong farmers living in Pathet Lao villages to learn about Communism and its ideas.

Many Hmong hoped the United States would help them. Instead of sending troops to Laos, the U.S. government offered to give the Hmong a chance to resettle in the United States. By 1990 more than 100,000 Hmong—including the Vangs— had left Southeast Asia to rebuild their lives in the United States.

Some Hmong refugee families were not allowed to move to the United States. Many of them were sent back from refugee camps to live in resettlement villages, which were built in remote areas of Laos with poor soil for farming.

In traditional village markets throughout Laos, vendors sell food, crafts, and other goods.

For thousands of years, the Hmong in Asia have survived by farming and raising animals. Living without electricity or indoor plumbing might seem difficult to someone growing up in the United States. But that's just how Xiong's parents, Toua and Kao, grew up in Laos.

Toua Vang was born in north central Laos in 1963. He describes his life in the village of Ban Pha Lo, where he was raised.

"My father had a prosperous farm. He owned 20 acres (8 hectares) of land and a small lake near Ban Pha Lo. We grew corn, rice, cucumbers, squash, sugarcane, and many other vegetables and fruits, including Hmong peaches grown from seeds our ancestors carried with them from China. We also raised cows, water buffalo, pigs, horses, and fish. My family all worked hard together to grow and prepare almost all the food we needed to survive. The only thing we had to buy in town was salt."

"As a young boy, I was expected to help with many chores around our farm. In the spring, I would help my father and other villagers clear new plots of land in the jungle to grow rice and corn. After we cut down the big trees, my father and our neighbors would pick a day to burn the new fields. When the day arrived, we made sure no one was in the fields and then set them on fire.

"Several weeks later, I would help my father dig holes in the ground for rice seeds. My mother and sisters followed behind us and dropped the seeds into the holes. After the seeds were planted, we usually weeded each field two times during the summer. Then we would harvest the rice in September or early October. Before we could eat the rice, my mother and my

In the lower valleys of Laos, many farmers plant rice in paddies, or wet fields (left). *Up in the high mountains, most Hmong farmers grow rice in dry fields.*

sisters would thresh and hull the rice at home with special wooden tools."

Toua continues, "I had two favorite jobs on the farm—feeding the fish we raised in our lake and riding the horse high up into the mountains to collect elephant grass. Elephant grass is very tall. It grows as high as the ceiling in an American house. We used it for many things. We dried the grass to make brooms and we fed the grass to my father's special bull. The more grass this bull ate, the stronger he became.

"As I cut the tall grasses and packed them onto the horse's saddle for the journey back down the mountain, I would dream about our bull winning the championship in the bullfights at the [Hmong] New Year's festival in November."

Like many Hmong in Laos, Toua only had the chance to go to school for a few years. "I attended the primary school in Ban Pha Lo for three years and then went to fourth grade in a larger village called Moueng Om. Moueng Om was about a four-hour walk from my home. On Sunday afternoons, I went to Moueng Om to study for the week. Every Friday night, I would walk back to Ban Pha Lo to help my family on the farm over the weekend."

Toua's life might have continued peacefully for many years on his family's farm. But the war in Southeast Asia changed his life forever.

When Toua was young, few Hmong children in Laos could attend school. Most young people had to work on the family farm or take care of smaller brothers and sisters.

25

General Vang Pao, the Hmong leader in the war against the Pathet Lao, directs warplanes to bomb Communist-held areas.

In 1974, when Toua was a fourth grader, the Vietnam War was coming to an end. But, Toua explains, the war against the Hmong in Laos was just beginning.

"Because we Hmong had helped the Americans, the Communists didn't like us. General Vang Pao, the Hmong general in charge of our military operations, dropped guns to my village by airplane. Every man and boy over 12 years old who wasn't away fighting was asked to take a gun and use it to protect the village from nighttime raids by the Communists.

"I was only 11 years old, just the age my son Xiong is now, but I got a gun, too. The gun was so long that it dragged in the dirt beside my feet. It was so heavy that I could only carry it for an hour or two at first. My first job was to go on night patrol once or twice a week around the village. Luckily, there were never any attacks on the nights I was on duty."

Toua continues his story, explaining that in 1975, the Pathet Lao Communists took over Laos. "My uncle had been a lieutenant in the CIA Secret Army. He soon realized that to survive, the Hmong had two choices— either to escape to the refugee camps in Thailand or to stay in Laos and continue to fight the Pathet Lao. My family decided to stay and fight."

Toua remembers guarding his village as a child during the war in Laos.

In an embroidered piece of artwork called a storycloth, Xiong's aunt sewed pictures of the Hmong people's struggle to survive during the war. Because the fighting was so heavy after 1975, many Hmong families fled to the jungle. This section of the storycloth shows how families cooked food over an open fire in the jungle. When they ran out of rice, the families had to survive on any roots, berries, and fruits they could find.

Toua's family and thousands of other Hmong families struggled to survive. When the fighting was far away, Toua's family lived on their farm in Ban Pha Lo. But when the fighting got close, his mother would gather her children and walk into the jungle. Sometimes they would sleep for only a night or two on the jungle floor and then return home. Other times, when the fighting was very intense, they built temporary houses out of wood from the trees in the jungle.

In the jungle, Hmong families suffered many hardships. Many people died from illness because doctors and medicine were not available. Others died from starvation because they were no longer able to grow their own food or raise animals. When they did have food, they weren't always able to cook it because Communist planes flying overhead could spot smoke from open fires.

Toua remembers, "One time my family hadn't eaten for a long time. We were so hungry. But then we found another family hiding in the jungle near us. They gave my mother some rice to cook. We were grateful for their help. For a little while, our stomachs were happy."

The jungle in Laos was deep and dense enough to hide Hmong families fleeing the Pathet Lao. But living in the thick rain forests also cut families off from reliable food sources and doctors.

 Xiong's mother, Kao Xiong, lived with her family in the jungle, too. But after several years, Kao's father decided his family couldn't survive in the jungle any longer. Like many other Hmong families, Kao's family chose to turn themselves in to the Pathet Lao and join Communist-controlled villages.

"We walked to a Pathet Lao village," explains Kao. "My father held up a piece of white cloth above his head, and we followed behind him. The Pathet Lao didn't shoot us, but we soon realized that surrendering to the Communists was a mistake. We didn't have our freedom anymore.

"Every morning we were told by the Pathet Lao leaders where to go, what to do, and how much to eat," continues Kao. "We Hmong didn't even have our own fields to farm anymore. Instead everyone had to farm the same fields together. And after we harvested the crop, the Communists divided up the crops so everyone had exactly the same amount of food—no matter how hard we had worked."

The Pathet Lao required all minority peoples—including the Hmong—to stay in their assigned villages. Anyone who tried to leave was taken back and usually punished for trying to escape.

(Right) *Hmong families trying to escape Laos had to cross the rushing Mekong River to reach Thailand.* (Above) *Kao holds a storycloth. Kao's name means "umbrella," a Hmong symbol of good luck that the family hoped would help them cross the river and escape Laos safely.*

After living in the Communist village for almost two years, Kao's father made the hardest decision of his life. He decided to take his family and escape the village, go back into the jungle, and walk more than 100 miles (160 kilometers) to the Mekong River. Kao will never forget this dangerous journey.

"About three days before we reached the river, my father told us to cut strips of bamboo. We trimmed each strip until they were each about three feet [one meter] long. Then we tied the strips together to form a triangle. We made one triangle for every person in my family. These bamboo triangles were going to be our life preservers to wear in the river. Without them we would drown in the strong currents of the Mekong River.

"Once my family reached the river, we waited quietly until the sun went down. My father, my brother, and my brother-in-law were the strongest swimmers in our family. Each one of them would lead a group across the Mekong River. I joined my father's group. There were about 20 of us just in my group. We put on our bamboo triangles, tied our triangles to one another with rope, and followed my father into the water. My brother and my brother-in-law's groups swam quickly across the dark river that night. But things didn't go so well for me and my father's group.

This piece of storycloth shows a group of Hmong refugees crossing the Mekong River.

Kao snuggles with Nancy and Toukee as she tells about the dangers her family faced in Laos.

"Almost as soon as we had gotten into the river, my father's bamboo triangle broke. We had to turn around, swim back to shore, and fix his preserver. We started again, but in no time my father's bamboo triangle had broken once again. Back we went to shore. This time we were getting very nervous. We knew that soldiers patrolled the riverbanks and shot people like us who were trying to escape Laos. What would happen to us?"

Kao's group tried getting into the water a third time. But her father's triangle broke again.

"When we returned to shore this time," continues Kao, "the Communist soldiers had finally spotted us. They opened fire. Gunshots were ringing all about. There wasn't time to think. I swam up alongside my father, and with the two of us in the lead, we guided our group toward the Thai side of the river.

"The current was very strong, but my father and I knew that if we didn't make it this time, we would be shot. My father prayed to our ancestors and asked them for help. Moments after he prayed, the river seemed gentler. Our group finally made it to the Thai shore, where my mother and the rest of my family were waiting. We had all escaped Laos, and we were finally safe."

Between 1975 and 1990, thousands of Hmong fled Laos and poured into refugee camps in Thailand. The families of both of Xiong's parents entered a camp called Ban Vinai in northeastern Thailand in 1980. The camp consisted of nine centers, or neighborhoods. In each center, most refugees lived in long bamboo houses shared by up to 10 families. They regularly received rations of rice, fish, and a few vegetables from the United Nations, an international organization that ran the camp. Women collected water at neighborhood water stations and cooked on wood fires inside their homes as they had in Laos.

Ban Vinai refugee camp was run by the United Nations.

Kao and other Hmong refugees sewed paj ntaub *for extra money, which they used to pay for English classes in the camp.*

A busy market stood at the center of the camp. An artificial lake and a soccer field had been built next to the market for recreation. The camp also had a hospital and health clinic, a school, and a sewage treatment plant.

For the first couple of years in Ban Vinai, Toua studied English and worked on Thai farms outside the camp. Later he got a job at the hospital and clinic. Meanwhile Kao studied at the camp school for a few years. She also sewed *paj ntaub,* an ancient form of Hmong embroidery.

While in the refugee camps, Hmong women created a new kind of paj ntaub called storycloths. These embroidered pieces tell the story of the Hmong people's journey from Laos to Thailand in search of freedom. Many Hmong seamstresses sent their work to relatives in the United States. The relatives would then sell the paj ntaub and send the money back to their families in the Thai refugee camps.

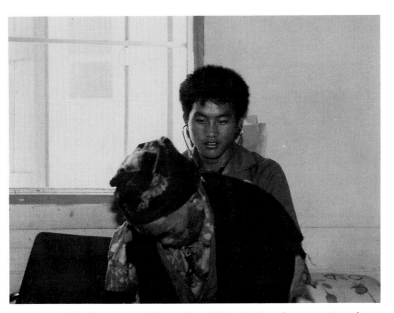

Toua worked as a medic at Ban Vinai. He also received ongoing training from foreign doctors and learned to diagnose illnesses and to prescribe medications. Toua is continuing his medical studies in Minnesota.

Hmong refugees could buy a variety of foods at the busy Ban Vinai market.

As a toddler, Xiong (top left) *loved to dance in the family's house in Ban Vinai. Xiong's grandmother, Mrs. Dou Vue, made Xiong this baby carrier* (bottom left) *so Kao could carry him on her back.*

Though Toua and Kao both lived in Ban Vinai, they did not meet until Kao got a job at the camp hospital where Toua worked. They married in 1982 and a year later, Xiong Pao Vang was born. Xiong was named during a special naming ceremony three days after his birth.

"During this ceremony," Kao explains, "we offer a chicken and some boiled eggs to the spirits. We also invite an elder to talk to the spirits and help us choose the right name for our child."

Xiong Pao Vang was named by his mother's father. Xiong's first name is his grandfather's last name. *Pao* means "power" in the Hmong language. By passing on his name to Xiong Pao Vang, Mr. Xiong was giving his grandson the power of his family's history.

Xiong doesn't remember much about living in Ban Vinai. "I was so small," he says. "But I do remember my friends the geckos." Geckos are small, friendly lizards that come out at night to eat mosquitoes.

"I remember waiting for the sun to go down and watching the geckos play on the walls of my family's bamboo house. Since we didn't have any electricity, I used to ask my grandmother for a flashlight. After it got dark, I would shine the light on the walls and search for the geckos. I guess I used to laugh when I found them. Sometimes my grandmother still teases me about the geckos!"

Toua says, "Although we had good jobs working in the medical clinic, Kao and I knew that life in the refugee camp was only temporary. After our second son, Xia, was born in 1985, we began making plans to leave Ban Vinai. There was no future for our kids in Laos or in the refugee camp."

Kao adds, "We wanted our children to have more than we did. Back in Laos, most Hmong kids didn't get to go to high school. Being Hmong means being free. We wanted our children to be free to have an education and to have a good life."

Toua, Xiong, and baby Xia pose for a photo in Ban Vinai. After Xia was born, Toua and Kao began making plans to move to the United States.

(Above) *Xiong enjoyed spending time with his grandmother and grandfather Vang in Ban Vinai. Xiong's grandfather eventually returned to Laos, where he died in battle. Xiong's grandmother, Mrs. Dou Vue, lives with the Vang family in Minnesota.* (Facing page) *This map shows the Vang family's journey from Laos to Minnesota.*

 Choosing to leave Ban Vinai for the United States was often a difficult choice for Hmong families. Many Hmong returned to Laos to fight the Communist government, hoping that one day all the Hmong people could return home. One of these Hmong fighters was Toua's father. He discouraged his family from leaving Ban Vinai. But many of the Vang's relatives, including Kao's older sister, had already resettled in California. They encouraged the Vangs to come to the United States.

Kao's older sister in California sponsored the Vangs to come to the United States. But first the family had to spend several months at Phanat Nikhom, a camp in central Thailand for refugees preparing to enter the United States. When the Vangs arrived at Phanat, they discovered that Kao was pregnant again—this time with twins.

After KaYing and Teng were born in 1986, the Vangs boarded a plane to the United States. On May 29, 1986, the Vangs and Toua's mother, Mrs. Dou Vue, arrived in Fresno, California. "Our new lives had finally begun," says Toua.

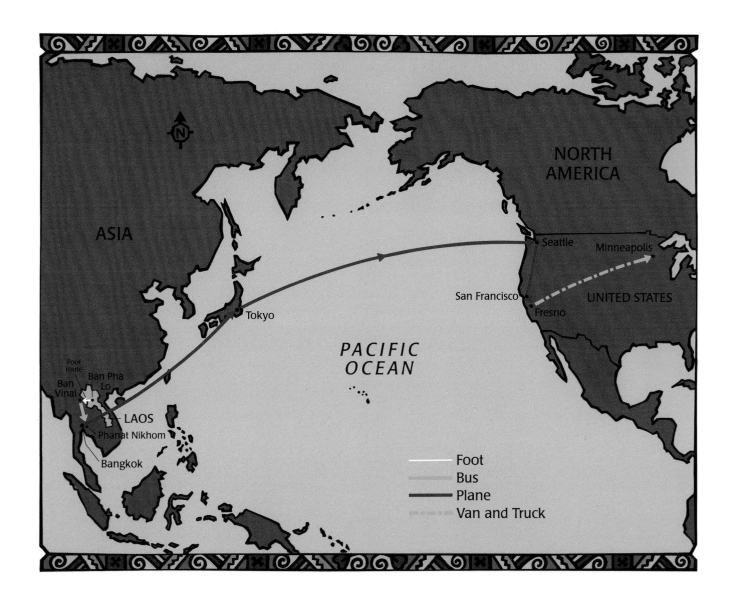

LEARNING PATIENCE

Many Hmong folktales are long and very complex. They are filled with animals, spirits, dragons, kings, and ordinary people. The following story is a tale that Xiong's uncle told when the Vangs still lived in California. Xiong says, "Now that I'm getting older, I see how the Hmong folktales can teach kids things. Sometimes my younger brothers are so impatient. Stories like "Learning Patience" teach them that sometimes it's better to wait to cross the street with the green light than to run across when the light's red."

Once upon a time, there were two brothers. One day while the brothers were out hunting, they each fell into a hole. Younger Brother fell into a dragon's hole and Older Brother fell into a rabbit's hole. Both holes were so deep, neither brother could climb out. But they each noticed that there were some bamboo grasses growing in the holes.

Older Brother said, "These grasses are too young. If we try to climb up the bamboo, it will break and we will fall back deeper into the hole. We have to be patient and wait for the grass to grow."

But Younger Brother was very impatient. He decided to try climbing on the young bamboo grass. Sure enough the grass broke, and he fell deeper into the hole. In fact, he ended up falling so far, he reached another world deep inside the earth far away from his family.

The world Younger Brother had entered was ruled by the foxes and populated by midgets. Younger Brother was put to work on one of the midget's farms. He began clearing the fields just as he had done back on his farm at the top of the earth. But soon the midgets became very angry because Younger Brother had cleared too much land.

The midgets said to Younger Brother, "King Fox will be very angry with us because we are only supposed to farm a small amount of the land. Please be careful, Younger Brother, or the foxes will eat you up." But Younger Brother wasn't afraid of foxes. He asked the midgets to take him to King Fox to talk about the land he'd cleared.

When they arrived at the king's home, they saw a rooster. Younger Brother was very hungry, so he killed the rooster and ate it. The midgets told Younger Brother that he was going to be in trouble because he had killed the king's rooster.

When King Fox came out and saw that Younger Brother had eaten his rooster, he was furious.

King Fox sent for his army of ants to fight Younger Brother and the midgets. The midgets were worried because they knew the ants would eat them up. They asked Younger Brother for help. Younger Brother told them not to worry. He had a plan.

Younger Brother and the midgets prepared 20 huge buckets of boiling water and dug a long gully in the ground. When the ants attacked and reached the gully, Younger Brother poured the hot water on the ants. Sure enough the ant army died.

Now that the midgets were safe from King Fox and his ant army, Younger Brother desperately wanted to get home to his wife. He went up to heaven to see the great god Shao to ask his advice. Shao told Younger Brother to tie two baby eagles in a tree with string. Younger Brother did as Shao asked.

The next day, the eagles' parents flew up to see Shao and ask him what to do to free their babies from the tree. Shao told the eagles to ask Younger Brother for help. The eagles flew back down to the midget world and found Younger Brother. Younger Brother promised to help them if they would promise to carry him up to the top of the earth.

The eagle parents agreed to the plan. But after Younger Brother freed the babies, the parents refused to help Younger Brother. So Younger Brother tied up the baby eagles again. Still, the parents did not keep their promise.

Finally, after Younger Brother had tied up the small birds a third time, the eagles agreed to help him. But first they needed to eat lots of cow and buffalo meat for the long journey up to the top of the earth. Younger Brother went hunting and brought them lots of meat. Soon the three began the journey up to earth.

Just before they reached the top of the earth, the eagles became very tired and almost fell back down. Younger Brother realized they needed more meat, so he offered them flesh from his own arm. Once the eagles ate Younger Brother's flesh, they were able to reach earth. Younger Brother happily jumped off the eagles' wings and found his wife and his brother waiting for him back on earth.

"I couldn't believe how easy life was in America when we first arrived," exclaims Kao. "By American standards, our first apartment in Fresno wasn't fancy. But compared to life in Laos or in the refugee camps, it was amazing! For the first time in our lives, we had electricity, indoor plumbing, and store-bought furniture. No more cooking over an open fire. No more dirt floors. No more walking outside to get water."

For Toua, having a car was the most valuable tool for life in the United States. "Imagine, I was 24 years old and I had never driven a car before!" he says. "Soon after we arrived, I began practicing driving. Then my brother-in-law lent me enough money to buy a used car for our family. Everything was so far apart in America. Having a car made such a big difference for our family."

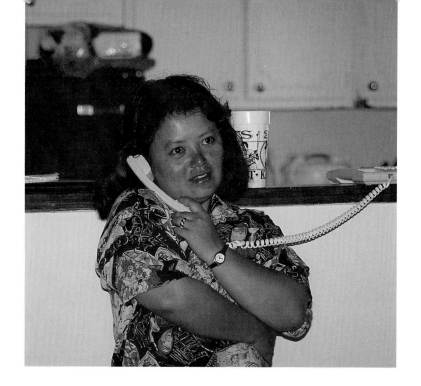

Xiong's parents like the new conveniences of life in the United States. Kao (left), who works at a telecommunications company, likes to be able to talk to friends and relatives by telephone. Toua (below) got his driver's license soon after arriving in the United States.

Xiong enjoys art class at Field Elementary School in Minneapolis, Minnesota.

Xiong was just three years old when his family arrived in California. He remembers that learning English was a big challenge. "At home we only spoke Hmong. So when I started kindergarten, I didn't know any English at all. It was really frustrating. I remember trying to ask my first-grade teacher for a pencil, and she thought I needed to go to the bathroom!"

Xiong soon mastered English. With help from his father, who had learned English in the refugee camp, Xiong studied hard each night. When he was able to read well enough, Xiong began helping his father tutor his younger brothers and sisters.

Toua (above), *who earned his high-school diploma in the United States, teaches the Hmong language to students in an after-school Hmong youth program. Xiong and Nancy* (left) *read and watch a video on television in the family's living room.*

Outside of school, Xiong loved to play soccer with his friends and take care of his roosters and hens. Xiong's grandmother helped him raise the animals in the family's large backyard.

"Every night before bed, I had to go outside and put the chickens in their shed," remembers Xiong. "One of the roosters really hated having to go to bed. He would climb up one of our trees, and I'd have to climb up after him, catch him, and carry him to the shed. In the mornings, they'd all wake up hungry. I'd get up really early and feed them corn."

Xiong's grandmother has also taught him a lot about Hmong culture. She is an herbalist. In Fresno she planted traditional herbs in the Vang's backyard and taught her grandson how to use the herbs to heal people. She has used her herbs to help Xiong many times.

Mrs. Dou Vue has a garden (left) *outside the family home where she grows herbs. As an herbalist, she uses powerful natural herbs to treat illnesses. Although her garden thrived in California, only a few of her plants grow well in Minnesota* (facing page), *where the climate is much colder.*

"Just last summer I had a high fever," says Xiong. "My grandmother made an offering of incense to the spirits and then picked some herbs from her garden. She chopped them, put them in a big leaf, heated them in the oven, and then wrapped the warm herbs around my wrist. It didn't take long before my fever went down."

In 1994 Xiong's parents decided to leave California and move to Minneapolis, Minnesota. They chose Minnesota because many of their relatives already lived there. They also knew that Minnesota offers good schooling and job opportunities. Leaving his neighborhood, friends, and roosters behind wasn't easy for Xiong. "I still miss California sometimes, especially in the winter!"

Xiong and his best friend, Nghia (left), discuss a school project. The two boys like to make up jokes, such as, "Why does a dog sound like a cow when it crosses the road? Because the dog has to moo to get across!" In the Hmong language, mus (pronounced "moo") means "to walk."

 Xiong's best friend in Minnesota is Nghia Lee. Xiong describes some of the games they play together at school. "At recess Nghia and I like to walk around outside and talk in our own secret language. We mix up Hmong and English words and make jokes. Hardly anyone else can understand us."

Xiong describes his classes. "Our homeroom teacher is Mrs. Soderlund. Every morning the kids take turns giving oral reports about news and current events. I got to report on an earthquake in Japan. But my favorite class is math. Me and two other kids do extra work every day in math so we can be ready for junior high. Right now we're doing algebra. I also love computer games. My favorite is Prince of Persia."

Twice a week after school, Xiong attends Hmong Youth Pride (HYP). Xiong explains, "HYP is a special program for Hmong kids. We do homework, study the Hmong language, play games, and do fun stuff like going swimming or taking field trips to the Mall of America."

Xiong and his friends in the Hmong Youth Pride program swim at a local pool.

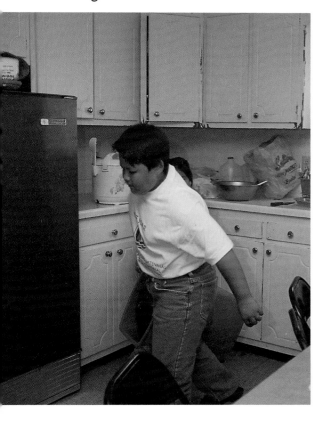

Xiong (below) *helps out at home by taking out the garbage and doing other chores. Gao* (right), *Xiong's uncle, is teaching his nephew about fixing cars.*

On weekends Xiong is always busy helping his family. He does chores, such as taking out the garbage. One of his favorite weekend activities is helping his Uncle Gao fix cars. As the oldest boy in his family, Xiong is also responsible for taking care of his siblings, especially his three younger brothers, Xia, Teng, and Toukee. "They're pretty naughty," Xiong remarks. "Sometimes I have to let them know who's boss."

Xiong and his father (above) *look over a homework assignment. Xiong, who is an excellent math student, does his homework after school each day, working to reach his dreams of becoming a doctor one day. Xiong* (left center) *and his brothers and sisters watch the animals at the zoo.*

Thousands of people attend the Hmong Soccer Tournament (left), a festival held in St. Paul, Minnesota, each summer. The festival provides Hmong families with an opportunity to play together and to celebrate their culture.

The Vangs (right) enjoy a traditional Hmong meal, including zaub iab *(vegetable soup),* zaub paj *(salted vegetable greens), rice, and chicken.*

Refugees can apply to be U.S. citizens after living in the United States for five years. In May 1994, exactly five years after he first arrived, Toua was sworn in as a U.S. citizen. Kao is studying for her citizenship exam. Once she becomes a citizen, the Vang children will automatically become U.S. citizens, too.

As parents, Toua and Kao try to balance Hmong traditions with the advantages of life in the United States. Toua says, "Our goal is to raise our children to be leaders for the next generations of Hmong here in America. We believe getting a good education in the American schools is very important for our children. But we also believe that our children should never forget where they've come from and what it means to be Hmong."

For example, Toua is teaching Xiong Hmong traditions for funerals and weddings. As the oldest son of the oldest son in his family, Xiong will one day be responsible for leading his family in these ceremonies. When his father's father died in Laos in 1992, Xiong went to California to participate in the ceremonies held in honor of his grandfather. Following his father's lead, Xiong helped cut and fold special paper into spirit boats. He also memorized many of the prayers for his grandfather's journey to the spirit world.

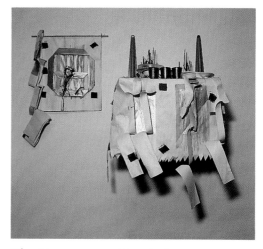

The Hmong practice their own religion, which is a form of animism. They believe that spirits live in the earth, in the sky, in animals, and in people. Most Hmong homes, including the Vang's, have altars where they keep incense and cutout paper to honor the spirits.

Kao, Nancy (left), *and KaYing* (right), *pose in traditional New Year's costumes. Mrs. Vue, the children's grandmother, embroidered the delicate skirts and hats.*

Another important Hmong tradition is the New Year's celebration. In Laos the festival took place outside on the first new moon of the traditional Hmong year.

The celebration would begin with the *lwm sub,* or pole ceremony. First the men in the village would cut down a tree, trim off all the branches except those at the top, and bring the tree into the village. After staking the tree to the ground, someone would tie a rope to the tree. A village elder would stand under the tree and offer a chicken to the spirits. Then he would sing a prayer asking the spirits to take the bad luck away with the old year and bring good luck in the coming year. Every family would take a turn walking under the rope and around the tree.

For unmarried teens, *pov pob,* or ball toss, was the most fun at the New Year's celebration. Xiong's grandmother, Mrs. Vue, recalls, "Back then New Year's was the time for young Hmong men and women to meet each other. We'd play pov pob together for hours. The boys would ask us to be their partners. Then we'd line up in the field—boys on one side and girls on the other. Then we'd toss the balls back and forth to our partners. Sometimes we'd tell stories or jokes. Many young people got married after New Year's. I met my husband playing pov pob many, many years ago!"

A close-up look at a traditional Hmong New Year's costume (right) *shows detailed patterns and delicate beadwork. Mrs. Vue* (far right) *is a skilled seamstress.*

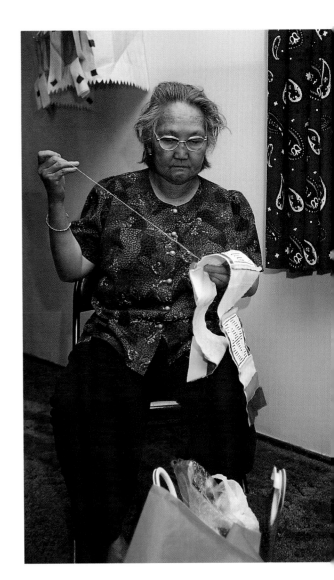

Mrs. Vue describes how she dressed her son for the celebration. "Back then I dressed Toua in black pants, black top, colored belts, and a black hat with bright colored tassels on the top. All the girls in the village would dress up, too. We used to wear pants like the boys, but today the girls and women wear skirts. The rich girls wore silver necklaces, too.

"We'd all sew special embroidered paj ntaub pieces to wear at the celebration. I've sewn several New Year's outfits for my granddaughters, KaYing and Nancy, here in America. They look so beautiful dressed up at New Year's."

Xiong watches other young people play pov pob, a ball-toss game, at the Hmong New Year's festival.

In Minnesota the Hmong usually celebrate the Hmong New Year on the weekend after Thanksgiving. Because there's usually snow on the ground, the ceremony takes place in St. Paul at the Civic Center, a large indoor arena in Minnesota's capital city, which lies close to Minneapolis.

The Hmong New Year means something very different for Xiong than it once did for his parents and grandparents. In the United States, only the women in Xiong's family dress in their traditional Hmong clothes. Xiong and his brothers wear jeans and sweatshirts, just like on any other day.

At the Civic Center, Hmong rock musicians perform Hmong American songs at one end of the arena. At the other end, several lines of young men and women play pov pob. At a small Hmong market, people can buy Hmong clothes, videos, and books. At the back, American hot dogs and pop are available.

Xiong, who is not old enough to be interested in the ball toss, walks around looking at Hmong videos and music tapes. Instead of buying something for himself, Xiong buys a balloon for his two-year-old cousin, who didn't get to go to the celebration.

"For me," observes Xiong, "the best thing about New Year's is seeing so many Hmong people together in the same place. I love walking around the Civic Center because it's filled with thousands of Hmong people. This is one of the few times when I don't look different from everyone around me out in public."

Browsing through the market section at the New Year's celebration, Xiong enjoys being around so many other people who share his culture.

The day after the New Year's festival, Xiong is up at 6:00 A.M. to watch cartoons and to challenge his younger brothers to a video game. "My brothers and I love playing video games. I can usually still beat them, but they're getting better all the time. We also like listening to the old Hmong stories my dad and uncles tell us sometimes," says Xiong.

Defining what it means to be Hmong or to be a refugee is hard for Xiong. He comments, "Hmong are just people, too."

And now that his family lives in the United States, Xiong doesn't really feel like a refugee anymore. "I'm glad we don't have to live in Laos. I'd be afraid my family would get killed," says Xiong. "But I do miss growing up around all the animals."

Xiong doesn't know exactly what he wants to do when he grows up, but he has several ideas. "I want a big house with enough bedrooms so my whole extended family can come stay with me whenever they want. I also want a big backyard so I can raise some animals."

Xiong's younger brothers Teng (left) *and Toukee* (right) *relax on the living room floor and draw pictures.*

Xiong (second from right) is happy living in the United States, but he also wants to carry on the Hmong traditions he has learned from his parents and grandmother.

Like his grandmother and his father, Xiong would also like to practice medicine. He wants to be a doctor. But for Xiong, that doesn't mean giving up his Hmong culture. "As the oldest son in my family, I know that someday I'll have to keep many of the Hmong customs alive for my parents and for my children.

"Even though I'll be an American citizen soon, I know I'll want my own son to speak the Hmong language and take care of me when I take my journey to heaven someday, too. I know my son will be happy here in America, too."

FURTHER READING

Goldfarb, Mace. *Fighters, Refugees, Immigrants: A Story of the Hmong.* Minneapolis: Carolrhoda Books, 1982.

Hmong Youth Cultural Awareness Project. *A Free People: Our Stories, Our Voices, Our Dreams.* Minneapolis: Hmong Youth Cultural Awareness Project, 1994.

Laos in Pictures. Minneapolis: Lerner Publications Company, 1996.

Shea, Pegi Deitz. *The Whispering Cloth: A Refugee's Story.* Honesdale, Pennsylvania: Boyds Mills Press, 1995.

Xiong, Blia. *Nine-in-One, Grr! Grr! A Folktale from the Hmong People of Laos.* Adapted by Cathy Spagnoli. San Francisco: Children's Book Press, 1989.

Zickgraf, Ralph. *Laos: Places and People of the World.* New York and Philadelphia: Chelsea House Publishers, 1991.

PRONUNCIATION GUIDE

Ban Pha Lo (BAHN PAH LOH)
Ban Vinai (BAHN vihn-EYE)
Dou Vue (DOO VOO)
Gao (GOW)
Hmong (MOHNG)
Kao (KOW)
KaYing (kah-YIHNG)
Laos (LAH-ohs)
lwm sub (LOO SHOO)
Mekong (may-KAWNG)
Moueng Om (MUHNG OHM)
Nghia (NEE-uh)
paj ntaub (PAHN DOW)
Pathet Lao (pah-TEHT LAH-oh)
Phanat Nikhom (pah-NAHT nee-KOHM)
pov pob (BAW BAW)
Shao (SHAH-oh)
Teng (TEHNG)
Thailand (TY-land)
Toua (TOO-ah)
Toukee (TOO-kee)
Vang, Xiong Pao (VANG, SHAWNG POW)
Xia (ZEE-uh)

*Hmong sounds are difficult to translate into English.
The pronunciations for Hmong words are approximations.

INDEX

ABOUT THE AUTHOR

Nora Murphy has worked in many Southeast Asian communities both internationally and in the United States. She began by teaching English to refugees in Massachusetts and later worked as a staff writer for several Southeast Asian community organizations in Minnesota. She is the author of two drug and crime prevention curricula for Hmong students, coauthor of the first study analyzing U.S. census data on the Hmong, and editor of a multicultural curriculum on Hmong culture and history. This is her first book for children. Ms. Murphy lives in St. Paul, Minnesota, with her husband and her son.

PHOTO ACKNOWLEDGMENTS

Cover photographs by © Nevada Wier (left) and Peter Ford (right). All inside photos by Peter Ford except the following: Scott Takushi, pp. 6, 7, 9, 35; Scott Takushi/Pioneer Press, pp. 8, 21, 24; © Brian Vikander, pp. 13, 25, 29, 32 (right); IPS, p. 17; Maurice Durand Collection of Vietnamese Art, Yale University Library, p.18; UPI/Corbis-Bettmann, pp. 19, 26, 31; © Nik Wheeler, p. 20; © Nevada Wier, p.22; Vang Family, pp. 36, 37 (left), 38 (top), 39, 40, 56; United Nations High Commissioner for Refugees, p. 37 (right). All artwork and maps by Laura Westlund.